LORIE TALBOTT

Management Toolbox

Build Stronger Teams, Inspire Growth, and Lead with Purpose

Copyright © 2024 by Lorie Talbott

All rights reserved. No part of this publication may be reproduced, stored or transmitted in any form or by any means, electronic, mechanical, photocopying, recording, scanning, or otherwise without written permission from the publisher. It is illegal to copy this book, post it to a website, or distribute it by any other means without permission.

Lorie Talbott asserts the moral right to be identified as the author of this work.

Lorie Talbott has no responsibility for the persistence or accuracy of URLs for external or third-party Internet Websites referred to in this publication and does not guarantee that any content on such Websites is, or will remain, accurate or appropriate.

Designations used by companies to distinguish their products are often claimed as trademarks. All brand names and product names used in this book and on its cover are trade names, service marks, trademarks and registered trademarks of their respective owners. The publishers and the book are not associated with any product or vendor mentioned in this book. None of the companies referenced within the book have endorsed the book.

First edition

This book was professionally typeset on Reedsy. Find out more at reedsy.com

Contents

Introduction	1
Chapter 1 Building the Foundation	3
Essential Skills for Effective Management	3
Understanding Your Leadership Style	7
Communication: The Cornerstone of Leadership	9
Chapter 2 Tools for Team Building	15
Recruiting and On boarding Tips	15
Fostering Collaboration and Trust	19
Managing Conflict Constructively	24
Chapter 3: Productivity and Performance	29
Setting SMART Goals	29
Time Management Strategies	32
Providing Feedback and Coaching	39
Chapter 4: Leadership in Action	43
Managing Remote and Hybrid Teams	43
Motivating and Inspiring Your Team	47
Decision-Making and Problem-Solving	51
Chapter 5: Personal Growth as a Manager	56
Embracing Continuous Learning	56
Developing Emotional Intelligence	59
Balancing Authority and Empathy	62
Conclusion	65
Creating Your Custom Toolbox	65
The Long-Term Impact of Effective Leadership	67

Introduction

Why Management Matters

Management is the backbone of every successful organization. Whether steering a small team or overseeing an entire department, managers play a pivotal role in shaping culture, driving performance, and achieving goals. A good manager doesn't just maintain processes; they inspire their teams, resolve conflicts, and create an environment where employees thrive.

For both new and experienced managers, the journey can be challenging yet incredibly rewarding. The skills and mindset you bring to the role determine not only your own success but also the success of those you lead. This book is here to guide you through that journey, offering practical tools and strategies to help you become the best manager you can be.

Overview of the "Management Toolbox" Concept

Imagine having a toolkit tailored specifically to help you navigate the complexities of management. That's the vision behind the *Management Toolbox*. Just as a craftsman uses different tools for different tasks, managers need a variety of approaches to tackle unique challenges.

From communication techniques and goal-setting frameworks to strategies for fostering team cohesion, this book is designed to be your go-to resource. Each chapter equips you with actionable tools that can be applied immediately, no matter your level of experience.

The Evolving Role of a Manager

The workplace has changed dramatically over the past few decades.

Remote work, diverse teams, and rapidly shifting markets have transformed the expectations placed on managers. Today's leaders must be adaptable, empathetic, and forward-thinking.

Gone are the days when management was solely about enforcing rules and tracking productivity. Now, the role demands a focus on collaboration, innovation, and the personal growth of team members. This evolution brings both challenges and opportunities—and with the right tools, you can navigate them confidently.

How This Book Will Help You Succeed

Whether you're stepping into a management role for the first time or looking to refine your leadership skills, *Management Toolbox* provides a structured, practical approach to management. This book will help you:

- Build strong relationships with your team.
- Set clear goals and measure success.
- Address common challenges with confidence and creativity.
- Cultivate a leadership style that is authentic and effective.

By the end of this book, you'll have a comprehensive toolkit to help you succeed in any managerial scenario. More importantly, you'll feel empowered to create a positive, high-performing work environment that benefits both your team and your organization.

Chapter 1 Building the Foundation

Before you can lead others effectively, you need to build a strong personal foundation. Great managers don't just manage, they lead by example, demonstrating the values and behaviors they want to see in their teams. This chapter covers the essential skills and self-awareness necessary to set the stage for successful management.

Essential Skills for Effective Management

Management is both an art and a science. While there are countless techniques and strategies, certain core skills form the foundation of effective management. Mastering these skills will help you handle day-to-day challenges with confidence and clarity.

1. Communication

Clear and effective communication is at the heart of good management. Whether you're sharing a vision, giving feedback, or listening to a team member's concerns, how you communicate determines the quality of your relationships and the efficiency of your team.

Key Practices:

- Be specific and concise in your messaging. Avoid jargon and ambiguity.

- Listen actively. Show your team that their input is valued by summarizing what you've heard and asking clarifying questions.
- Adapt your communication style to suit different audiences, whether it's senior leadership or front line employees.

Example:

Imagine you're leading a project where deadlines are tight. Instead of saying, "We need to finish this quickly," you specify, "This project needs to be completed by Friday at 5 PM to meet the client's expectations. Each team member should update their task progress by 3 PM daily." This eliminates confusion and ensures everyone is aligned.

2. Decision-Making

Managers make decisions daily, from small process improvements to major strategic shifts. Effective decision-making requires balancing logic, intuition, and collaboration.

Key Practices:

- Gather and analyze relevant data before making decisions.
- Involve your team when appropriate to gain diverse perspectives.
- Be decisive but flexible—don't be afraid to adjust course if new information emerges.

Example:

Suppose your team has proposed two potential marketing campaigns, one targeting young adults and the other focusing on families. Rather than choosing based on personal preference, you analyze customer data and discover that families are the larger demographic for your product. Based on this insight, you communicate this information to the team and decide to prioritize the family-focused campaign.

3. Time Management

Time is one of a manager's most valuable resources. The ability to prioritize effectively can mean the difference between progress and stagnation.

Key Practices:

- Use tools like to-do lists, calendars, and project management software to stay organized.
- Delegate tasks that others can handle, freeing yourself to focus on higher-level responsibilities.
- Set boundaries to avoid burning out and ensure time for strategic thinking.

Example:

Your calendar is packed with meetings, but you have an important presentation to prepare. Instead of trying to do it all, you delegate smaller, less critical tasks—such as scheduling follow-ups or creating reports—to a reliable team member. This frees you to focus on the high-priority work.

4. Emotional Intelligence (EI)

Your ability to understand and manage both your emotions and the emotions of others can significantly impact team morale and performance. Emotional intelligence fosters trust and collaboration.

Key Practices:

- Practice self-awareness by reflecting on your emotional triggers and responses.
- Show empathy by acknowledging others' feelings and perspectives.
- Maintain composure under pressure to set a positive tone for your team.

Example:

A team member seems disengaged during meetings. Instead of reprimanding them, you request a one-on-one time frame to check in with them. They share that they're struggling with a personal issue. By offering support and asking if there is anything you or the team can help with, you demonstrate empathy, openness, and build trust.

5. Adaptability

In today's fast-paced work environment, adaptability is non-negotiable. Managers must be open to change and quick to pivot when circumstances require it.

Key Practices:

- Embrace change as an opportunity for growth, rather than a disruption.
- Encourage your team to develop a growth mindset, viewing challenges as learning experiences.
- Stay informed about industry trends and innovations to stay ahead of the curve.

Example:

During a product launch, unexpected supply chain delays occur. Instead of panicking, you quickly organize a brainstorming session with your team to find alternatives. By shifting resources and re-negotiating deadlines with key partners, you minimize the delay's impact and maintain team morale.

Mastering these essential skills will lay a solid foundation for your management journey. With these tools in place, you'll be ready to develop a leadership style that is authentic, effective, and uniquely yours.

CHAPTER 1 BUILDING THE FOUNDATION

Understanding Your Leadership Style

Every manager brings their own unique approach to leadership. Your leadership style shapes how you make decisions, interact with your team, and handle challenges. Understanding your natural tendencies allows you to leverage your strengths and address areas for growth.

In this section, we'll explore common leadership styles and how to identify the one that fits you best. We'll also look at how to adapt your style to meet the needs of your team and organization.

1. Common Leadership Styles

Managers often fall into one or more of these leadership categories, depending on their personality and workplace dynamics:

- **Authoritative:** Focused on vision and direction, authoritative leaders inspire others by setting a clear path forward.
- **Democratic:** These leaders prioritize collaboration and value team input before making decisions.
- **Coaching:** Coaching leaders focus on developing individuals and fostering long-term growth.
- **Laissez-Faire:** Hands-off leaders trust their team to work independently, stepping in only when necessary.

2. Identifying Your Style

To identify your leadership style, reflect on how you handle these scenarios:

- When making decisions, do you consult others, or do you prefer to decide independently?
- How do you respond when your team struggles with a task?

- What motivates you to lead—achieving goals, build relationships, or guiding others?

Example:
Maria, a newly promoted manager, always believed in collaboration. During her first team meeting, she asked for input on setting priorities for the quarter. While some team members appreciated the opportunity to contribute, others felt overwhelmed without clear guidance. Realizing this, Maria took a leadership assessment and discovered her democratic style. She learned to adapt by providing more structure when needed, ensuring all team members felt supported while maintaining a collaborative approach.

3. Adapting Your Style to the Situation

Effective managers don't rely on one style in every situation—they adapt to what their team or the circumstances require.

- **When speed is critical:** An authoritative approach can help provide quick, decisive leadership.
- **When fostering innovation:** A democratic style encourages creative input and fresh ideas.
- **When developing talent:** Coaching works best to support individual growth and confidence.

Example:
Jake managed a team of software developers working on a tight deadline. Initially, he leaned into his coaching style, asking the team how they thought they could solve a bottleneck in the project. But as the deadline loomed, he realized they needed decisive direction. Jake quickly outlined a step-by-step plan, assigning clear tasks to each developer. His ability to shift to an authoritative style kept the project

on track and delivered results on time.

4. Leveraging Self-Awareness to Lead

Knowing your leadership style is only part of the equation. Self-awareness allows you to recognize when your natural tendencies are helpful—and when they might hinder your effectiveness.

Example:

Aisha, a laissez-faire leader, thrived when working with her highly skilled marketing team. But when she took over a new team of less experienced employees, her hands-off approach led to confusion and missed deadlines. By reflecting on feedback from her team, Aisha recognized the need for more structure. She gradually introduced check-ins and clear workflows while still encouraging independence, creating a balance that helped her team succeed.

Understanding and adapting your leadership style is an ongoing process. By building self-awareness and remaining open to feedback, you can ensure your leadership approach evolves with your team's needs.

Communication: The Cornerstone of Leadership

Clear and effective communication is the foundation of successful leadership. As a manager, your ability to articulate ideas, listen actively, and foster open dialogue directly impacts team performance, trust, and morale. Strong communication isn't just about delivering messages, it's about ensuring understanding and alignment.

1. Master the Art of Active Listening

Active listening goes beyond simply hearing what someone says, it involves fully understanding their perspective, emotions, and needs.

Key Strategies:

- **Eliminate Distractions:** Put away your phone, close your laptop, and give your full attention to the speaker.
- **Paraphrase and Reflect:** Summarize what you've heard to confirm understanding. For example: "So, you're saying the project timeline is causing delays because of resource availability. Is that correct?"
- **Ask Clarifying Questions:** Dive deeper with open-ended questions like, "Can you give me more details on that?"

Example:

During a one-on-one meeting, a team member shares concerns about workload. Instead of jumping to conclusions, the manager actively listens, paraphrases the concern, and asks follow-up questions. This approach helps uncover specific issues and creates an opportunity to develop tailored solutions.

2. Adapt Your Communication Style

Not everyone processes information the same way. Adapting your communication style to suit the needs of different team members enhances clarity and connection.

Key Strategies:

- **For Analytical Thinkers:** Focus on data and logic to support your points.
- **For Creative Thinkers:** Use stories or visuals to convey ideas.
- **For Hands-On Learners:** Provide practical examples or demonstrations.

Example:

When introducing a new project management tool, the manager tailors the explanation:

- For data-driven team members, they highlight analytics features.
- For visual learners, they create a demo.
- For hands-on learners, they provide a step-by-step guide.

3. Encourage Open Dialogue

Creating a culture of open communication empowers team members to share ideas, voice concerns, and contribute to problem-solving.

Key Strategies:

- **Ask for Input:** Regularly seek feedback and ideas from your team.
- **Create a Safe Space:** Ensure team members feel comfortable speaking up without fear of judgment.
- **Facilitate Team Discussions:** Use meetings to encourage collaboration and brainstorming.

Example:

In a weekly team meeting, the manager invites everyone to share updates and discuss roadblocks. By encouraging contributions, the team feels valued and more invested in outcomes.

Real-Life Example:

In our repair facility, we used highly specialized and expensive equipment to calibrate repaired units. One day, a piece of this critical equipment had to be sent out to the manufacturer for servicing and calibration. When it returned and was in the process of being re-installed, it slipped and crashed onto the concrete floor.

Within 10 minutes of the incident, the managers were in my office.

Their opening words were familiar: *"We know you're not going to want to hear this, but you need to know."* That was often our way of bracing for bad news. They proceeded to explain the situation.

My immediate response was, *"Was anyone hurt or injured?"* When they assured me that everyone was fine and that only the equipment had taken the damage, I expressed my gratitude: *"Thank you for coming to me so quickly. I know that wasn't easy, and I truly appreciate your trust in me."*

In that moment, I praised them for their honesty and quick action. Together, as a team, we formed a plan to address the situation. We were able to secure a loaner unit while the damaged equipment was sent back for repairs, which took approximately three months.

This experience remains one of my proudest moments as a manager—not because of how we solved the problem, but because my team trusted me enough to bring the issue forward without hesitation.

Takeaway:

Take a moment to reflect on a time when you experienced an *"it's bad"* situation. How did you handle it? Could you have done something differently? Re-evaluating your approach to such moments is challenging but invaluable. You're here, reading this book, because you're looking for insights to grow. Moments like these can be some of your greatest opportunities for growth and connection as a leader.

4. Be Clear and Concise

Effective communication avoids misunderstandings and keeps everyone on the same page. Clarity ensures that your message is understood, and conciseness respects everyone's time.

Key Strategies:

- **Structure Your Message:** Begin with the main point, provide supporting details, and conclude with any required actions.
- **Avoid Jargon:** Use straightforward language that everyone can

understand, especially when discussing complex topics.
- **Check for Understanding:** Ask questions like, "Does that make sense?" or "Do you have any questions about this?" to confirm clarity.

Example:

Instead of saying, *"We need to address the workflow issues as soon as possible,"* say, *"By Friday, I'd like us to identify the top three bottlenecks in the workflow and propose solutions to address them."* This ensures clarity between the task and the deadline.

Real-Life Example:

In our repair shop, we would often hear the phrase, *"It's broken."* Our immediate follow-up question was, *"What is it not doing that you're expecting it to do?"* If that didn't provide the clarity we needed, we asked them to show us exactly what they did so we could replicate the issue.

While your specific situation may be different, the principle remains the same: dig deeper beyond the surface-level description of *"it's broken"* to clearly define the issue. Only then can it be effectively addressed.

5. Leverage Non-Verbal Communication

Non-verbal cues—body language, tone of voice, and facial expressions—play a significant role in how your message is received.

Key Strategies:

- **Maintain Eye Contact:** Show engagement and build trust.
- **Use Open Body Language:** Avoid crossing your arms or appearing closed off.
- **Be Mindful of Tone:** Ensure your tone matches the intent of your message.

Example:

During a performance review, a manager maintains a warm tone and open posture while delivering constructive feedback, ensuring the team member feels supported rather than criticized.

6. Key Tips for Effective Communication

- **Tailor Your Approach:** Adjust your communication style based on the audience and situation.
- **Be Transparent:** Honest, open communication builds trust and credibility.
- **Practice Empathy:** Understand and acknowledge others' perspectives.

Strong communication is a cornerstone of effective leadership. By mastering these skills, you can inspire trust, foster collaboration, and drive your team toward success.

Chapter 2 Tools for Team Building

A manager is only as strong as their team. Building a cohesive, motivated, and skilled team starts with hiring the right people and ensuring their transition into the organization is seamless. In this section, we'll explore practical tools for recruiting and on boarding, fostering collaboration, and managing conflict effectively.

Recruiting and On boarding Tips

1. Recruiting for Fit and Potential

When interviewing candidates, it's important to assess not only their technical skills but, more importantly, their values, motivations, and potential to adapt and fit into your team. Thoughtful, open-ended questions are key to understanding who the individual is and how they approach challenges, decisions, and teamwork. The goal is to uncover the candidate's core values and determine how well they align with your team's dynamics and culture.

1. Sample Interview Questions:

- *"Can you describe a time when you faced a significant challenge and how you handled it?"* This question helps uncover the candidate's problem-solving abilities, resilience, and approach to decision-making. However, it's crucial to dig deeper into the outcome, not just the challenge itself.

For example, if the challenge involved a difficult client situation, the manager should follow up with:

- *"What was the final result of the situation?"*
- Did they achieve success, or were there elements beyond their control? Observe their emotional reaction—does it indicate investment in outcomes or detachment?
- *"Did you handle the resolution on your own, or did you seek assistance from others?"*
- Both outcomes are positive. If they handled it themselves, it shows independence and quick thinking. If they sought assistance, it indicates awareness of their limits and a willingness to leverage resources for success.
- *"Looking back, is there anything you would have done differently or that should have been done differently?"*
- Do they show adaptability and a commitment to improvement, or do they dismiss the opportunity to reflect and grow?

Encourage candidates to share stories from any aspect of their lives, not just work. This broadens your understanding of their resourcefulness and values. For instance, a story about organizing a neighborhood fundraiser under tight deadlines might demonstrate leadership, adaptability, and the ability to deliver results. With the bonus you discover what they are passionate about, and it can have a very positive effect to put them at ease.

2. Key Insights about the answers:
If a candidate shares that they handled an irate client by first

actively listening to their concerns, then coordinating with a team to implement a solution that met the client's needs, this shows ownership, collaboration, and a focus on outcomes. On the other hand, if they describe a challenge where someone else had to step in to resolve the issue, it could highlight areas for growth.

- *"Tell me about your proudest moment. This can be work related or something in your personal life."*

This open-ended question provides insights into the candidate's values. For example, if they share a story about coaching their child's little league team, it could indicate that they value family, teamwork, and perseverance. Whether they emphasize winning or the joy of seeing the team work together, their response offers clues about their priorities and leadership potential.

- *"If money were no problem, you have everything you need, money, health, you're happy, and your family is happy, what would you like to do?"*

This question helps reveal the candidate's passions, long-term goals, and what truly motivates them. Are they driven by helping others, pursuing knowledge, or perhaps creating something meaningful? Their answer may provide a glimpse into their personal values and aspirations, which can inform you how they will align with your team's mission and culture.

3. Understanding who this person is:

- Guide each conversation toward understanding the candidate's role in achieving outcomes, and the lessons they took away from the experience.

- Pay attention to their ability to reflect and articulate lessons learned. A candidate who can self-assess is more likely to adapt and grow in the role.
- Encourage non-work examples. Challenges from other areas of life, such as personal projects or volunteer efforts, can reveal just as much about their abilities.

Recruiting effectively means understanding the candidate as a whole—how they think, what they value, and how they handle real-world challenges. By using thoughtful, purposeful questions and diving into the details of their responses, you can make informed decisions based on evidence, not assumptions.

4. Creating a Seamless On boarding Experience

A new hire is excited, ready for the adventure, eager to learn, and wants to be part of a thriving hive of workers. Don't let disorganization, time constraints, or lack of preparation dampen their excitement for joining your team. As a manager, your time is valuable, and while you care about your team, you often find yourself pulled in different directions. That's why we recommend assigning a mentor to the new employee for the first 30 days—or even longer, if the job is complex.

One-on-one mentoring provides the best of both worlds. Your new hive member feels valued and supported, not left alone to fend for themselves. They begin to form a bond with their mentor, someone who has a clear understanding of the role, responsibilities, and expectations of the job. A mentor can easily integrate the new team member into the group's dynamics, ensuring they feel welcomed from day one.

A mentor does more than answer questions—they serve as a guide, equipping the new hire with the resources and confidence they need to succeed. More importantly, the mentor serves as a direct access point for questions and support. When challenges arise, the mentor is likely to notice them early and share feedback with the manager, enabling proactive problem-solving and ensuring the new hire stays on track.

By assigning a mentor, you bring that new valued team member into the fold with the same excitement and openness they're showing by coming on board. This not only sets the foundation for a thriving, cohesive team but also creates an environment where everyone feels supported and empowered to contribute their best.

Recruiting and on boarding effectively not only build strong individual team members but also set the stage for a culture of trust and collaboration. These processes are the foundation for long-term success in team building.

Fostering Collaboration and Trust

Collaboration and trust are the cornerstones of a successful team. Without them, even the most skilled individuals can struggle to work cohesively and achieve common goals. As a manager, it's your responsibility to cultivate an environment where team members feel comfortable sharing ideas, supporting one another, and trusting their colleagues to deliver.

1. Building a Collaborative Environment

Collaboration doesn't happen automatically; it requires intentional effort to create a culture where team members feel valued and heard.

Strategies for Collaboration:

- **Encourage Open Communication:** Create opportunities for team members to share their ideas, concerns, and feedback. For example, regular brainstorming sessions or "open-door" policies can help foster a sense of inclusion.
- **Leverage Individual Strengths:** Understand each team member's

unique skills and assign tasks that play to their strengths. This not only enhances productivity but also builds confidence.
- **Set Shared Goals:** Ensure everyone understands how their work contributes to the team's overall objectives. A shared sense of purpose strengthens collaboration.

2. Building Trust Within Your Team

Trust is the glue that holds a team together. Without it, collaboration falters, and morale suffers. Building trust requires consistency, transparency, and respect.

Strategies for Building Trust:

- **Lead by Example:** Demonstrate integrity, accountability, and fairness in all your actions. Your behavior sets the tone for the team.
- **Show Vulnerability:** Admit it when you don't have all the answers and be open to learning from your team. This humanizes you and encourages trust.
- **Acknowledge Contributions:** Recognize and celebrate individual and team achievements. People are more likely to trust a leader who values their efforts.

3. The Rope Trick: An Exercise in Collaboration and Trust

To emphasize the importance of collaboration and trust, managers can use a simple but powerful exercise called *The Rope Trick*. This activity demonstrates how teams rely on trust, communication, and participation to succeed.

How It Works:
Setup:

- Arrange the team in a line, with each person spaced an elbow-length

apart.
- Stretch a rope across the group and have each person hold it in their hands.

Blindfolds:

- Blindfold every participant. They must now rely on communication and teamwork to accomplish the task.

The Task- Goal:

- Instruct the group to form the rope into a circle within 5 minutes (deadline).
- Observe the dynamics as natural leaders and followers emerge.

Adding Complexity:

- During the exercise, tap two or more participants on the shoulder and quietly instruct them to drop the rope, remove their blindfolds, and step back from the group. This simulates team members stepping out of tasks or becoming disengaged. (Individual members are out sick, vacation, disengaged. Teams not delivering on time – impacting the goal)
- After some time, tap the quietest participant on the shoulder and instruct them to remove their blindfold. They now have permission to guide the rest of the team to complete the task.

Completion:

- Once the circle is formed, remove the blindfolds and begin a discussion with all participants.

Discussion Points:

- **How did it feel to be blindfolded?** Participants might express feelings of confusion, frustration, or uncertainty, as well as trust their team to get the job done.
- **What happened when people vanished from the rope?** Participants often notice how missing team members affect the group's success, mirroring real-world scenarios where disengagement or lack of communication create challenges.
- **How did it feel to follow the quiet participant?** This highlights the value of all voices, especially those who might typically stay in the background.
- **Lessons Learned:**

-Trust and communication are essential for achieving goals.
  -Every team member has value and deserves to be heard.
  -Leaders can emerge from unexpected places.

This exercise is not only a powerful metaphor but also an engaging way to drive home the importance of collaboration and trust within a team.

Now let's reflect on the Manager's role in the Rope Trick Exercise.

- Did you clearly state the objectives <u>before</u> the exercise began, giving the team time to digest the information. (goal setting, clear vision)
- Did you ask for <u>input</u> from the team their thought on the best approach as to how to accomplish the task. (engaging and planning)
- Did you give your team the tools and knowledge to be <u>successful</u>. Letting them know there will most likely be some bumps along the way but together we can accomplish the goal.

One final note when teaching this method to the team: I applied a lesson I learned as a leader by clearly stating the goal and objective before beginning. The key rule was that once their hands touched the rope, the blindfolds had to go on. Interestingly, the team decided to form a circle before putting on the blindfolds, feeding the rope from one hand to another until the rope completed the circle. This approach was perfectly acceptable, as the ultimate goal was to form a circle with the rope. Trust was still achieved, knowing the next person was there to receive the rope, and communication was reinforced as they guided each other on how far the rope had traveled.

The lesson I learned is that when you provide a clear vision ahead of the task and allow the team to plan for the challenge, they often come up with creative solutions—freeing you to focus on other priorities. While this is a simple example, challenge yourself to see how this approach could be applied effectively in your daily life.

4. Encouraging Peer-to-Peer Support

Trust isn't just about the manager—it also needs to exist between team members. Encourage peer-to-peer support to create a stronger, more cohesive team.

Strategies for Peer Support:

- **Promote Cross-Training:** Allow team members to learn from one another by sharing skills and knowledge. This not only builds trust but also enhances flexibility within the team.
- **Create Buddy Systems:** Pair newer employees with experienced team members to facilitate knowledge sharing and build connections.
- **Celebrate Team Wins:** Highlight moments where the team worked together to achieve success, reinforcing the importance of collaboration.

Fostering collaboration and trust is an ongoing process that requires patience, consistency, and creative approaches like *The Rope Trick*. By creating an environment where team members feel valued, respected, and supported, you lay the foundation for a high-performing and cohesive team.

Managing Conflict Constructively

Conflict is an inevitable part of any team dynamic. When managed effectively, it can lead to greater understanding, improved relationships, and innovative solutions. As a manager, your goal is not to avoid conflict but to address it constructively and turn it into an opportunity for growth.

1. Understanding the Roots of Conflict

Conflict often arises from misunderstandings, differing goals, clashing personalities, or—most commonly—wrong assumptions. Assuming someone's intent, goals, or perspective without confirmation can lead to unnecessary confusion and escalation. Recognizing the root cause of the conflict is the first step in resolving it effectively.

Common Sources of Conflict:

- **Communication Breakdowns:** Misinterpretations or lack of clarity in communication can lead to disagreements.
- **Competing Priorities:** Team members may have conflicting goals or expectations.
- **Personality Clashes:** Differences in work styles or temperaments can create tension.
- **Unverified Assumptions:** Jumping to conclusions about another person's intent, actions, or capabilities without seeking clarifica-

tion.

Example:
Imagine a team member, Chris, assumes another colleague, Jamie, missed a deadline because they didn't prioritize their piece of the project effectively. Chris vocalizes their frustration, which Jamie interprets as an attack on their work ethic. Jamie was waiting on additional input from a client to complete the task. This entire conflict stemmed from an unverified assumption and could have been avoided with a simple question: *Help me understand what caused the delay?"* This phrasing seeks clarification without assigning blame, fostering understanding rather than escalating tension.

2. Steps for Managing Conflict Constructively
Step 1: Create a Safe Space for Dialogue
Encourage open communication by providing a neutral and safe space where all parties can express their concerns without fear of judgment or retaliation. Usually, this is best achieved in a one-on-one setting behind closed doors to avoid embarrassing anyone or creating a spectacle in front of other team members. This approach ensures that participants feel comfortable and respected, paving the way for honest discussions.

Step 2: Address Assumptions Directly
When conflict arises, explicitly ask each party what assumptions they've made about the other. Encourage them to focus on facts and clarify their understanding.

Step 3: Listen Actively
Focus on understanding each person's perspective before proposing solutions. Paraphrase their concerns to show that you're listening and validate their feelings.

Step 4: Identify Common Goals
Shift the focus from individual grievances to shared objectives.

Highlight how resolving the conflict benefits the entire team.

Step 5: Develop a Collaborative Solution
Involve all parties in brainstorming potential solutions. This ensures buy-in and fosters a sense of shared responsibility.

Step 6: Follow Up
Monitor the situation to ensure the resolution is effective and that relationships are improving.

3. Conflict Resolution Exercise: The Perspective Swap
This exercise helps team members see the situation from another person's point of view, fostering empathy and understanding.

How It Works:

1. **Identify a Conflict Scenario:** Choose a real or hypothetical conflict relevant to the team.
2. **Assign Roles:** Have each participant take on the perspective of someone else involved in the conflict.
3. **Discussion:** Ask participants to explain the conflict from their assigned perspective, including the challenges they face and their goals.
4. **Debrief:** After the discussion, have the participants reflect on what they learned about the other person's viewpoint.

Discussion Points:

- Did seeing the conflict from another perspective change your understanding of the situation?
- How can empathy contribute to more effective conflict resolution?
- What steps can be taken to ensure all voices are heard in future conflicts?

3-a. Conflict Resolution Exercise: Assumptions and Facts

This exercise helps participants identify and challenge their own assumptions while focusing on facts to resolve conflict.

How It Works:

1. **Identify a Conflict Scenario:** Use a real or hypothetical conflict that involves unverified assumptions.
2. **List Assumptions:** Have each party write down the assumptions they've made about the other person or situation.
3. **Compare with Facts:** Facilitate a discussion where participants compare their assumptions with actual facts. For example: Assumption: "Jamie doesn't care about deadlines." Fact: "Jamie was waiting on additional client input to complete the task."
4. **Debrief:** Reflect on how assumptions influenced the conflict and what could have been done differently.

Discussion Points:

- How often do we make assumptions without verifying them?
- How can we prevent assumptions from escalating conflicts in the future?
- What tools or habits can we develop to seek clarity before reacting?

4. Key Tips for Conflict Management

- **Stay Humble:** Ask questions without blame. Help me understand how I can help? Are there other alternatives we need to explore? I am having a hard time figuring out the best course of action what are your thoughts?
- **Stay Neutral:** As a manager, avoid taking sides. Your role is to

facilitate resolution, not to assign blame.
- **Focus on Behavior, Not Personalities:** Address specific actions or decisions, not personal traits.
- **Encourage Respect:** Set clear expectations that all discussions should remain respectful, even during disagreements.
- **Know When to Intervene:** Some conflicts may be resolved on their own, while others require your direct involvement. Recognize when your input is needed.

Effectively managing conflict is about turning challenges into opportunities for growth. By addressing disagreements constructively and fostering understanding among team members, you strengthen relationships and enhance the overall performance of your team.

Chapter 3: Productivity and Performance

Setting SMART Goals

Goals are the foundation of productivity and performance. Without clear, actionable objectives, teams can struggle with direction, priorities, and accountability. SMART goals—Specific, Measurable, Achievable, Relevant, and Time-Bound—provide a framework that ensures clarity and focus, helping both individuals and teams succeed.

What Are SMART Goals?

SMART is an acronym that ensures goals are well-defined and actionable:

- **Specific:** Goals should be clear and precise. Avoid vague or ambiguous language.
- **Measurable:** Define success with quantifiable metrics. How will progress and achievement be tracked?
- **Achievable:** Ensure the goal is realistic given the resources, time, and capabilities available.
- **Relevant:** Align the goal with broader team or organizational objectives.
- **Time-Bound:** Set a deadline or time frame to maintain urgency

and focus.

Example of a SMART Goal:
"Increase customer satisfaction scores by 10% within the next six months by implementing a new feedback system and providing additional customer service training that focuses on the customer feedback concerns."

How to Create SMART Goals with Your Team
Step 1: Start with the Big Picture
Discuss the team's overarching goals or the organization's strategic objectives. How can individual or team goals contribute to these larger aims?

Step 2: Break It Down
Work with team members to break these objectives into smaller, SMART goals. This makes them more manageable and easier to track.

Step 3: Involve the Team
Collaborate with your team when setting goals. This fosters ownership and ensures alignment with their capabilities and motivations.

Step 4: Document and Communicate
Write down the goals and share them with everyone involved. This creates accountability and ensures everyone is on the same page.

Step 5: Monitor and Adjust
Regularly review progress and make adjustments with the team as needed. Listen to their challenges and collaborate on solutions. This keeps the team on track and allows for flexibility if circumstances change. Open dialogue during reviews fosters trust and ensures that the team feels supported in overcoming obstacles or adapting to new priorities.

Goal-Setting Exercise: The SMART Map

This exercise helps teams practice setting SMART goals together.
How It Works:

- **Divide Into Small Groups:** Break your team into smaller groups and provide each group with a specific challenge related to your work. For example, "Improve team communication."
- **Define a SMART Goal:** Each group must turn the challenge into a SMART goal. Encourage them to ask:

-What is the exact outcome we're trying to achieve? (Specific)
-How will we measure success? (Measurable)
-Can we realistically accomplish this? (Achievable)
-Why is this goal important to our team? (Relevant)
-When will this be completed? (Time-Bound)

- **Present and Refine:** Have each group present their SMART goal to the rest of the team. Provide constructive feedback and refine the goals together.

Key Tips for Setting SMART Goals

- **Stay Flexible:** While goals should be time-bound, allow room for unforeseen challenges or opportunities.
- **Celebrate Wins:** Acknowledge and celebrate when goals are achieved to keep morale high and reinforce positive behavior.
- **Review What Went Right:** When goals aren't fully met, treat it as an opportunity to reflect and grow. Review what went right and identify ways to continue improving. Focusing on both successes and areas for growth ensures a balanced perspective, encourages progress, and motivates the team to strive for even better results in

the future.
- **Balance Ambition with Realism:** Encourage the team to aim high but remain grounded in what's achievable.

SMART goals not only provide clarity but also create a sense of purpose and direction. By aligning individual efforts with team objectives, you set the stage for improved productivity and meaningful results.

You can also think of SMART goals like a map. The goal is your desired destination. Laying out the route of how you're going to get there. (break it down) What type of transportation are used to get there, what supplies will you need to take, and regular updates to make sure you are on track with the timeline.

Time Management Strategies

Time is one of the most valuable resources for managers and their teams. Effective time management ensures that priorities are met, deadlines are achieved, and productivity remains high. As a manager, mastering your own time while helping your team optimize theirs is key to long-term success.

1. Prioritize Tasks Effectively

Not all tasks are created equal. Learning to prioritize ensures that critical objectives are met while less urgent tasks don't derail progress.

Key Strategies:

Use the Eisenhower Matrix: Divide tasks into four categories:

1. **Urgent and Important:** Do these immediately.
2. **Important but Not Urgent:** Schedule these for later.
3. **Urgent but Not Important:** Delegate these.
4. **Neither Urgent nor Important:** Eliminate these tasks.

CHAPTER 3: PRODUCTIVITY AND PERFORMANCE

Focus on High-Impact Work: Concentrate on tasks that align with your team's goals and deliver the most significant results.

Example:

Emails can quickly consume a manager's time, pulling focus away from high-priority tasks. A manager should request that team members format their emails clearly, placing the manager's name in bold on the left-hand side and specifying the actions needed. For example, "**[Manager's Name]**: Please approve this budget by Friday." This ensures that actionable items are easily identifiable.

Often, managers find themselves copied on long email chains with no clear need for their input. By asking for clarity upfront and reviewing only actionable emails during focused time blocks, managers can prevent email overload. Additionally, it's essential to recognize that most emails are low-priority items. Take care of the "big boulders" first—high-impact, time-sensitive tasks—and address the "pebbles" (low-priority items) as time allows.

2. Delegate Effectively

Many managers struggle with delegation, fearing that tasks won't be done as well or as quickly. However, delegation not only lightens your workload but also empowers your team and builds their skills.

Key Tips:

- Match tasks to team members' strengths and areas for growth.
- Provide clear instructions and expectations.
- Trust your team and resist micromanaging—allow them to approach tasks in their own way.

Balance Delegation and Support:

While micromanaging is counterproductive, periodic check-ins are essential to ensure that the team member is not overwhelmed and has the support they need. These check-ins provide an opportunity to address questions or obstacles that the team members may not have been able to resolve on their own.

All too often, managers delegate and then leave the team members to flounder without offering guidance or feedback. Instead, aim to:

- Provide constructive feedback to help them refine their approach.
- Celebrate their progress and acknowledge their effort.
- Praise the team member for taking on the task, especially if it's outside their comfort zone, and express your appreciation for their willingness to learn and grow.

Example:

A manager juggling multiple deadlines realized they were spending hours creating reports that a team member could handle. By delegating the task and providing clear guidance up front, the manager freed up time to focus on strategic planning. They scheduled a quick check-in after the first report was completed to ensure everything was on track and to address any questions. When the task was successfully completed, the manager praised the team member's attention to detail and initiative, reinforcing their confidence and fostering a sense of accomplishment.

3. Avoid Multitasking

While multitasking may seem productive, research shows it often reduces efficiency and increases errors. Focusing on one task at a time ensures quality, accuracy, and a greater sense of accomplishment.

Key Strategies:

- **Focus on One Task at a Time:** Prioritize tasks and give your full attention to one item before moving on to the next.

- **Use Time-Blocking:** Dedicate specific periods to individual tasks, ensuring uninterrupted focus.
- **Limit Distractions:** Turn off notifications, close unnecessary tabs, and set boundaries during focused work periods.

Block Time for Yourself:

It's perfectly acceptable to block time on your calendar for meetings with yourself. Marking these slots as "busy" signals to others that your time is allocated and provides the space you need to focus on critical tasks without interruptions. This simple practice reinforces the importance of prioritizing your own work and helps you avoid falling into reactive multitasking.

4. Encourage Team Time Management

As a manager, helping your team adopt effective time management practices can improve productivity and reduce stress. Introducing proven techniques can empower your team to work more efficiently.

Key Strategies:

1. **Weekly Planning Meetings:** Hold brief meetings to set priorities and align key deliveries.
2. **Shared Calendars:** Use shared scheduling tools to improve coordination and visibility.
3. **Introduce Time Management Techniques:** Share tools and methods, such as the Pomodoro Technique and Task Batching, to enhance focus and productivity.

The Pomodoro Technique

The Pomodoro Technique is a time management method designed to help people stay focused and avoid burnout by breaking work into short,

concentrated intervals. Each interval is traditionally 25 minutes long, followed by a short break. These intervals are known as "Pomodoros."
How It Works:

1. Choose a task to work on.
2. Set a timer for 25 minutes.
3. Work on the task until the timer rings.
4. Take a 5-minute break. Get up and stretch, look outside, sing a song. The break should relieve the stress on your body and mind.
5. Repeat the cycle for four Pomodoros, then take a longer break (15-30 minutes).

Why It Works:

The Pomodoro Technique encourages focused effort in manageable chunks, making it easier to tackle large tasks. The breaks help refresh the mind, reducing fatigue and maintaining productivity throughout the day.

Task Batching

Task batching involves grouping similar tasks together and completing them during a designated block of time. This reduces context switching and increases efficiency by allowing you to focus on one type of activity at a time.
How It Works:

- Identify tasks that are similar in nature, such as:

Emails and communications
    Administrative work
    Creative tasks like writing or designing

CHAPTER 3: PRODUCTIVITY AND PERFORMANCE

- Schedule specific time blocks in your day for each category of tasks.
- During those blocks, focus solely on that category and avoid distractions.

Why It Works:

By working on related tasks in batches, you minimize the mental effort required to shift between different types of activities. For example, instead of checking emails throughout the day, you could dedicate 30 minutes in the morning and another 30 minutes in the afternoon to clear your inbox. This structured approach helps you stay focused on your highest priorities.

Let's look at this in a bit of a simpler example. An individual has been tasked with creating five letters for various clients. Noting that the letters have a very similar theme and just a few changes for each client are needed. Once the letters are completed, they will need to have the signature (s) of the appropriate individuals and then mailed. Two options are available to complete the task.

1. First option type up one letter once it is completed seek the appropriate individuals signature, then place it in the envelope, address it, seal it and run to the post office to mail it. Return to work and begin the second letter.
2. Second option type up all 5 letters. Once they are completed obtain the signatures for all the letters, place them in their respective envelopes, address them, run to the post office and mail them. The task is now complete.

You're probably laughing a bit right now because who would ever pick option one. Very ineffective and wears a person out just thinking about it. My challenge to you is self-evaluation. Are there times when you find yourself in option one and can it be moved to option two scenario.

These strategies ensure that your team has the tools to manage their time effectively. Encourage them to experiment with these techniques and find what works best for their individual workflows. By empowering your team with clear methods, you can foster a culture of productivity and balance.

Time Management Exercise: The Daily Reflection

This exercise helps individuals identify patterns in their time usage and make improvements.

How It Works:

1. **Track Your Time:** For one week, have team members log how they spend their time each day, including interruptions.
2. **Reflect on Patterns:** At the end of the week, review logs to identify where time is being spent effectively and where adjustments could be made to minimize distractions or optimize workflows.
3. **Plan for Change:** Encourage each person to develop a strategy to enhance their time management by focusing on high-priority tasks and addressing any inefficiencies identified during the reflection.

Discussion Points:

- What surprised you about how you spent your time?
- What small changes can you make to improve your time management?
- How can the team support each other in minimizing interruptions?

5. Key Tips for Time Management

- **Model Good Practices:** As a manager, demonstrate effective time management to inspire your team.
- **Set Boundaries:** Protect your time for strategic tasks by limiting unnecessary meetings or interruptions.
- **Review Progress Regularly:** Periodic reviews help ensure that time is being spent on the right priorities.

Time management is about working smarter, not harder. By mastering your own time and helping your team do the same, you create an environment where goals are met efficiently, and stress is minimized.

Providing Feedback and Coaching

Feedback and coaching are essential tools for improving individual and team performance. When done effectively, they can build confidence, enhance skills, and foster a growth-oriented culture.

1. The Art of Giving Feedback

Feedback should be constructive, actionable, and delivered in a way that motivates rather than discourages.
Key Principles:

- **Be Specific:** Avoid vague statements like "You need to do better." Instead, say, *"I think the report will be much more powerful if we include X, Y, Z data points. Is that something we can do?"* This phrasing is collaborative and constructive, focusing on actionable improvements without sounding critical.
- **Balance Positive and Constructive Feedback:** Acknowledge

successes while addressing areas for improvement.
- **Avoid the "but":** Saying, *"You did X, Y, Z great, but we still need A, B, C,"* can unintentionally negate the positive feedback. Instead, separate the two with more encouraging language.
- **Start with Their Perspective:** Before offering constructive feedback, ask the individual if they think anything could have been done better. Often, they are already aware and more receptive to discussing improvements.

Example:

- Manager: "Your presentation was engaging and well-organized. Do you think there's anything we could tweak for next time?"
- Team Member: "I think the Q&A section was rushed."
- Manager: "That's great! We're on the same page. No worries—we're growing and figuring everything out, and this is part of the process. Let's allocate more time for that section next time."

This approach fosters collaboration and shows you're focused on growth rather than pointing out flaws.

- **Be Timely:** Provide feedback as close to the event as possible to ensure relevance and clarity

2. Coaching for Growth

Coaching focuses on long-term development by helping team members set goals, overcome challenges, and reach their potential.

Key Coaching Strategies:

- **Ask Open-Ended Questions:** Encourage self-reflection with questions like, "What do you think went well?" or "What would you

do differently next time?"
- **Provide Guidance, Not Answers:** Help them find their own solutions rather than dictating what to do.
- **Set Development Goals:** Work with team members to set goals that align with their strengths and areas for improvement.

Example:

If a team member is struggling with delegation, a coaching conversation might go like this:

- Manager: "I noticed you've been handling most of the project work yourself. What's been challenging about delegating tasks to the team?"
- Team Member: "I'm worried they won't get it done right."
- Manager: "I understand. Let's discuss how you can provide clear instructions and build trust with the team so that delegation becomes easier."

Feedback and coaching are essential tools for improving individual and team performance. When done effectively, they can build confidence, enhance skills, and foster a growth-oriented culture.

3. Feedback and Coaching Exercise: The "STAR Technique"

This exercise helps managers practice by giving clear and actionable feedback using the STAR (Situation, Task, Action, Result) technique.

How It Works:

1. Situation: Describe the context. ("During last week's team meeting…")
2. Task: Explain what was required. ("You were asked to present the project timeline…")

3. Action: Highlight what they did. ("You provided a detailed overview but omitted key deadlines.") We all want to use "but" and hear it is. It takes time and practice to think differently. Let's take this sentence and rethink it. "You provided a great detail overview. Do you think something was missing though?" If they don't come up with it on their own, then something like "We probably need those deadlines, so everyone is on the same page."
4. Result: Explain the outcome. ("This caused some confusion about deliverables. Let's adjust the presentation approach next time to include the deadline details.")

Practice: Have managers role-play feedback scenarios using STAR to ensure clarity and effectiveness. Remember your words are very powerful and use them wisely.

Effective feedback and coaching inspire team members to perform at their best and continuously grow. By mastering these skills, you cultivate a culture of openness, trust, and high performance.

Chapter 4: Leadership in Action

Managing Remote and Hybrid Teams

The rise of remote and hybrid work environments has transformed the way teams operate. While these models offer flexibility and access to a broader talent pool, they also present unique challenges in communication, collaboration, and maintaining team cohesion. As a manager, adapting your leadership style to meet these challenges is essential.

1. Foster Clear and Open Communication

Clear communication is the foundation of any successful team, but it becomes even more critical in remote and hybrid environments where face-to-face interactions are limited.

Key Strategies:

- **Establish Regular Check-Ins:** Schedule meetings on a consistent basis so everyone knows when to discuss progress, challenges, and goals. We recommend a minimum of once a week, but if there are many moving parts, 2 or 3 check-ins per week may be necessary. Additionally, ensure team members know they can reach out to coordinate one-on-one meetings whenever needed. This open-

door policy fosters trust and ensures that issues or questions are addressed promptly.
- **Use Multiple Communication Channels:** Combine email, messaging apps, video calls, and collaborative platforms to keep everyone connected. Additionally, if needed, have a tracking system that can be used to create tickets, set priorities, and give visibility to the progress that is being made.
- **Clarify Expectations:** Clearly define deliverables, deadlines, and roles to ensure everyone understands what is expected. Confirm understanding by getting each individual's thumbs up that they are on board. If challenges arise with a specific group, offer to set up a smaller meeting to discuss the issues and brainstorm solutions together. Engagement is key—ensure everyone acknowledges their role in the deliverables and feels committed to contributing to the team's success.

Example:
A remote marketing team uses a combination of weekly video calls, daily updates, and shared project management tools to stay aligned and maintain transparency.

2. Build Team Cohesion
Maintaining a sense of connection and camaraderie is challenging when team members are not physically together.
Key Strategies:

- **Encourage Team Bonding Activities:** Organize virtual coffee breaks, trivia games, or team-building workshops.
- **Celebrate Successes:** Acknowledge milestones, big and small, through virtual shout outs or digital awards.
- **Promote Inclusivity:** Ensure remote team members feel equally

valued by involving them in discussions and decisions.

Example:
A hybrid software team celebrates project launches with a virtual "happy hour," ensuring both in-office and remote members can join. This helps build rapport and creates a shared sense of accomplishment.

3. Support Flexibility and Work-Life Balance
One of the advantages of remote work is flexibility, but it can also blur the boundaries between work and personal life.
Key Strategies:

- **Encourage Breaks:** Remind team members to take regular breaks to recharge.
- **Set Boundaries:** Model healthy boundaries by limiting after-hours communication.
- **Provide Resources:** Offer tools or stipends for home office setups to ensure a comfortable and productive work environment.

Example:
A manager noticed a team member sending emails late at night and scheduled a conversation to discuss work-life balance. Together, they implemented strategies to manage workloads during regular hours, improving the employee's well-being and productivity.

4. Track Performance Without Micromanaging
Remote work requires trust and accountability. While it's important to track progress, excessive oversight can damage morale.
Key Strategies:

- **Focus on Outcomes:** Evaluate performance based on results rather

than hours logged.
- **Use Project Management Tools:** Several software platforms allow for transparent progress tracking without constant check-ins.
- **During Regular Check-Ins:** Use scheduled check-ins to provide meaningful feedback, recognize achievements, and discuss any support needed. These reviews should focus on actionable insights and creating opportunities for productive discussions rather than consuming the manager's time with casual updates.

Example:

A remote team tracks their progress using a shared dashboard where tasks are updated in real-time. The manager reviews this weekly and uses it as a basis for discussions, ensuring that the time spent is focused on addressing specific needs, celebrating progress, and identifying solutions for any challenges.

5. Key Tips for Managing Remote and Hybrid Teams

- **Adapt Leadership Styles:** Flexibility in how you manage and communicate with each individual is crucial.
- **Leverage Technology:** Use tools that enhance productivity and connection, but avoid overloading the team with too many platforms.
- **Be Accessible:** Maintain an open-door policy, even virtually, so team members feel comfortable reaching out with concerns or ideas.

Managing remote and hybrid teams requires intentionality, adaptability, and a focus on connection. By implementing these strategies, you can create a cohesive and productive team environment, no matter where your team members are located.

CHAPTER 4: LEADERSHIP IN ACTION

Motivating and Inspiring Your Team

Motivation is the fuel that drives teams to achieve their goals, while inspiration keeps them striving for excellence. As a manager, your role is to cultivate a sense of purpose, foster enthusiasm, and create an environment where team members feel valued and empowered.

1. Understand What Motivates Each Individual

Every team member is unique, with different values, goals, and sources of motivation. Taking the time to understand what drives each person allows you to tailor your approach.

Key Strategies:

- **Ask Questions:** During one-on-ones, ask questions like, "What do you enjoy most about your work?" or "What would you like to accomplish this year?"
- **Recognize Intrinsic vs. Extrinsic Motivation:** Some team members are motivated by personal growth and achievement (intrinsic), while others respond to rewards and recognition (extrinsic).

Example:

A manager discovers that one team member thrives on learning new skills, while another is driven by public recognition. By offering training opportunities to the first and celebrating the second's achievements during team meetings, both are motivated in ways that resonate with them.

2. Create a Vision That Inspires

People are more motivated when they feel connected to a larger purpose. Share a vision that excites and unites your team.

Key Strategies:

- **Articulate the "Why":** Explain how each task or project contributes to the team's or organization's bigger picture.
- **Make It Personal:** Show how their work impacts others—whether it's customers, colleagues, or the community.
- **Celebrate Milestones:** Highlight progress toward the vision to keep the momentum going.

Example:
When launching a new product, a manager emphasizes how the team's work will solve a real-world problem for customers. By sharing customer stories and positive feedback, the manager reinforces the team's impact and inspires pride in their work.

3. Recognize and Reward Achievements

Recognition is a powerful motivator. When team members feel their efforts are noticed and appreciated, they're more likely to stay engaged.
Key Strategies:

- **Make Recognition Specific:** Instead of a generic "good job," acknowledge the specific actions or outcomes.
- **Use Both Public and Private Recognition:** Celebrate achievements during team meetings, but also send personal notes or have one-on-one conversations.
- **Offer Rewards:** For significant milestones, consider small rewards like gift cards, extra time off, or team lunches.

Example:
After a successful project delivery, the manager hosts a team lunch to celebrate and publicly highlight each member's unique contributions. For a particularly impactful team member, the manager sends a personal thank-you note expressing appreciation for their dedication.

CHAPTER 4: LEADERSHIP IN ACTION

Real-Life Example:

Every Friday, we evaluated whether we had met our repair goals, which measured how many repairs were completed during the week. With 115 employees, taking everyone to lunch wasn't feasible. Giving extra time off felt hollow and didn't truly embrace the idea of celebrating as a team. We needed a solution that was engaging, cost-effective, included everyone, and could be done during work hours without impacting home life.

The Solution:

Games. Everyone enjoys playing games! We brainstormed simple, interactive games like charades, tic-tac-toe, board games, and card games. The idea was to create an environment where everyone could relax, bond, and have fun. To make it work, we divided the employees into teams of five, which meant organizing 23 different game stations, each featuring a unique game. This was achievable with a little planning.

To encourage team bonding across departments, we added a twist: a deck of cards. Each team member drew a card and proceeded to the designated game station for that card, where they'd meet and play with participants from other teams. Soon, the air was filled with laughter, chatter, and energy as games were played across the center.

Fridays transformed into something to look forward to: "Have we met our goal yet? How much more do we need? What team can I help to get us there?" As excitement grew, we added small perks, like a free beverage and snack before the games began. Eventually, we purchased a popcorn machine, which became a favorite low-cost treat.

One week, we even celebrated by attending a local high school baseball game together and cheering them on. These moments didn't just celebrate success—they built camaraderie and created lasting memories.

Takeaway:

Celebrations and rewards don't have to be complicated or expensive. Take the time to brainstorm creative ideas and listen to what your team values. Simple gestures like games, snacks, or shared experiences can strengthen bonds, boost morale, and leave a lasting impact on your team. I still smile when I think back on those Fridays—proof that even small celebrations can make a big difference.

4. Empower Your Team

Giving team members autonomy and ownership over their work increases engagement and motivation.

Key Strategies:

- **Encourage Initiative:** Give team members the freedom to propose ideas or solve problems independently.
- **Provide Resources and Support:** Ensure they have the tools and training needed to succeed.
- **Trust Your Team:** Avoid micromanaging and show confidence in their abilities.

Example:

A manager empowers a team member to lead a new initiative, offering guidance as needed but allowing them to take full ownership. The result is a more confident, motivated employee who feels trusted and valued.

5. Key Tips for Motivation and Inspiration

- **Be Consistent:** Regularly check in to ensure team members stay motivated over time.
- **Model Enthusiasm:** Your energy and passion are contagious—lead by example.
- **Focus on Strengths:** Recognize and leverage each team member's unique talents.

Motivating and inspiring your team is an ongoing process that requires understanding, recognition, and empowerment. By fostering a sense of purpose and belonging, you can create a high-performing team that is driven to succeed.

Decision-Making and Problem-Solving

Effective leadership requires the ability to make sound decisions and solve problems efficiently. Whether addressing immediate challenges or planning long-term strategies, decision-making and problem-solving skills are essential for navigating complex team dynamics and achieving goals.

1. Embrace a Structured Approach

Using a structured method for decision-making ensures clarity and reduces emotional bias.

Key Strategies:

- **Define the Problem:** Clearly articulate the issue at hand and its impact on the team or organization.
- **Gather Information:** Collect relevant data, input from team members, and any historical context.
- **Explore Options:** Brainstorm possible solutions, considering both immediate fixes and long-term impacts.
- **Evaluate and Decide:** Weigh the pros and cons of each option before choosing the most effective course of action.
- **Implement and Review:** Execute the decision and assess its effectiveness over time.

Real-Life Example:

A repair facility faced a common but frustrating challenge in its intake area: processing boxes of units for repair. The paperwork accompanying each unit was inconsistent and often disorganized. Some paperwork was wrapped tightly around the unit with too many rubber bands, and critical information wasn't visible. This created delays and frustration for the intake team.

One team member approached their lead with a question: *"Is there a better way to handle this?"* The lead saw an opportunity to streamline the process and began brainstorming with the team. They focused on defining the *desired* best way to receive paperwork and units to ensure efficiency.

After some brainstorming and testing, they developed a mock-up:

- **The New Standard:** Fold the paperwork so that the customer information is visible on the outside, place it flat on the face of the unit, and secure it with a single rubber band. This setup left the barcode on the back of the unit accessible for quick scanning, allowing intake to verify information without removing the rubber band.

The process worked perfectly internally—but how could they encourage external locations to adopt it?

Driving Change Externally:

The team first implemented the new process for repaired units being shipped back to the locations, demonstrating its efficiency firsthand. Next, they created a step-by-step flyer illustrating the new inbound process.

Implementation Steps:

1. Flyers were included in every outbound shipment for 30 days.
2. Store managers received an email with the flyer, asking them to

CHAPTER 4: LEADERSHIP IN ACTION

adopt the new standard.

As more locations adopted the process, the intake team saw dramatically faster processing times. For locations that resisted the change, managers were invited to the facility for a *show-and-tell* session. Seeing the efficiency firsthand—and realizing their shipments weren't part of the streamlined system—motivated even the reluctant locations to comply.

Takeaway:

Sometimes, improving a process requires clear communication, collaboration, and persistence. By defining a structured approach, demonstrating its value, and engaging stakeholders, even widespread operational challenges can be overcome. This example illustrates how small, thoughtful changes can lead to significant efficiency gains—and how teamwork and strategic communication drive results.

2. Foster Collaborative Problem-Solving

Team involvement in decision-making not only leads to better outcomes but also boosts morale and ownership.

Key Strategies:

- **Leverage Team Expertise:** Involve team members with relevant skills or knowledge.
- **Encourage Diverse Perspectives:** Invite input from across the team to uncover blind spots or innovative ideas.
- **Facilitate Discussions:** Use tools like brainstorming sessions or SWOT analysis (Strengths, Weaknesses, Opportunities, Threats) to guide discussions.

Example:

When designing a new workflow, a manager facilitates a brainstorming session with the team. By encouraging open dialogue, they uncover a solution that balances efficiency with flexibility, satisfying both client and team needs.

3. Manage Risk and Uncertainty

Not all decisions come with clear outcomes. As a leader, managing risk and uncertainty is part of the job.

Key Strategies:

- **Identify Risks:** Assess potential challenges or consequences associated with each option.
- **Create Contingency Plans:** Prepare for potential setbacks by outlining alternative approaches.
- **Be Decisive:** Avoid analysis paralysis—commit to the best option based on available information.

Example:

While launching a new product, a manager identifies potential supply chain delays as a risk. They develop a contingency plan that includes alternative suppliers, ensuring minimal disruption if issues arise.

4. Empower Team Members to Solve Problems

Encourage your team to take ownership of challenges and develop their problem-solving skills.

Key Strategies:

- **Ask Guiding Questions:** Help team members think critically by asking questions like, "What options have you considered?" or "What might the impact of this choice be?"
- **Provide Tools and Training:** Offer frameworks like root cause analysis or decision trees to support problem-solving.
- **Celebrate Successes:** Acknowledge when team members solve

problems independently to reinforce their confidence.

Example:
A team member proposes a cost-saving measure for a recurring expense. The manager asks guiding questions to refine the plan and then supports the team members in implementing it, resulting in both savings and personal growth for the employee.

5. Key Tips for Decision-Making and Problem-Solving

- **Stay Calm Under Pressure:** Approach challenges with composure to inspire confidence in your team.
- **Be Transparent:** Share the reasoning behind your decisions to build trust and understanding.
- **Learn from Outcomes:** Whether a decision succeeds or falls short, use it as a learning opportunity to improve future processes.

Decision-making and problem-solving are at the heart of effective leadership. By combining structure, collaboration, and adaptability, you can lead your team through challenges and make confident decisions that drive success.

Chapter 5: Personal Growth as a Manager

Embracing Continuous Learning

The best leaders understand that growth is an ongoing process. In today's rapidly evolving workplace, staying informed and adaptable is essential for maintaining your effectiveness as a manager. Continuous learning not only enhances your skills but also sets an example for your team to follow.

As Fabienne Fredrickson wisely said, *"The day you plant the seed is not the day you eat the fruit."* Growth takes time, patience, and consistent effort. Every step you take toward learning and self-improvement builds the foundation for future success.

1. Cultivate a Growth Mindset

A growth mindset encourages curiosity, adaptability, and resilience. Managers who embrace this mindset see challenges as opportunities to learn and improve.

Key Strategies:

- **Seek Feedback:** Actively ask for input from peers, mentors, and your team. Questions like, "What can I do better?" or "How can I support you more effectively?" show your commitment to growth.

- **Learn from Setbacks:** View mistakes as valuable learning experiences rather than failures. Reflect on what went wrong and how to improve moving forward.
- **Stay Open to Change:** Embrace new ideas, technologies, and processes to remain adaptable in a dynamic environment.

Example:
After a challenging project where deadlines were missed, a manager conducts a post-mortem with the team. By listening to feedback and reflecting on their own role, they identify areas for improvement and implement changes for the next project.

2. Invest in Professional Development

Staying up-to-date with industry trends and enhancing your skill set demonstrates leadership and ensures you remain effective in your role.

Key Strategies:

- **Attend Workshops and Seminars:** Gain insights from experts and expand your network.
- **Pursue Certifications or Courses:** Explore opportunities to deepen your expertise in areas like leadership, project management, or technical skills.
- **Join Professional Communities:** Engage with industry groups or forums to stay connected and learn from peers.

Example:
A manager enrolls in a leadership course focused on emotional intelligence. The skills they gain help them improve team dynamics, making them a more effective leader.

3. Encourage Peer Learning

Learning doesn't always have to come from formal settings. Engaging with peers is a valuable way to exchange knowledge and broaden perspectives.

Key Strategies:

- **Create Managerial Peer Groups:** Form a group of managers across departments to share experiences and solutions.
- **Shadow Other Leaders:** Spend time observing how other managers handle their teams to learn different approaches.
- **Participate in Cross-Training:** Engage in training sessions outside your immediate expertise to gain a broader understanding of your organization.

Example:

A manager joins a monthly peer group where leaders discuss challenges and share strategies. In one session, they learn a new approach to time management that significantly improves their team's productivity.

4. Key Tips for Continuous Learning

- **Make Time for Learning:** Dedicate time each week to reading, attending webinars, or exploring new tools.
- **Apply What You Learn:** Integrate new knowledge or techniques into your daily work to reinforce learning.
- **Lead by Example:** Demonstrate a commitment to growth by sharing your learning journey with your team.

By embracing continuous learning, you embody the truth of Fabienne Fredrickson's words: consistent effort and growth today will yield the fruits of success tomorrow. Stay curious, adaptable, and committed to improvement—not just for yourself but for the team and organization you lead.

Developing Emotional Intelligence

Emotional intelligence (EI) is the ability to recognize, understand, and manage your emotions while also being attuned to the emotions of others. As a manager, developing EI is critical for building trust, fostering collaboration, and leading with empathy. Teams thrive when leaders demonstrate emotional awareness and connection.

1. The Core Components of Emotional Intelligence
Self-Awareness:
The ability to recognize and understand your own emotions and how they affect your thoughts and behaviors.

- **Practice Reflection:** Take time to assess your emotional responses in challenging situations.
- **Seek Feedback:** Ask colleagues or mentors for insight into how your emotions impact your leadership.

Self-Regulation:
The ability to manage your emotions, especially in high-stress or difficult situations.

- **Pause Before Reacting:** Take a moment to breathe and collect your thoughts before responding.
- **Set Personal Boundaries:** Protect your energy and mental clarity by managing time and avoiding unnecessary stressors.

Empathy:

Understanding and sharing the feelings of others to build deeper connections.

- **Listen Actively:** Pay attention to what is being said and unsaid during conversations.
- **Put Yourself in Their Shoes:** Consider how a decision or situation might feel from the other person's perspective.

Social Skills:
The ability to build and maintain healthy relationships and resolve conflicts effectively.

- **Communicate Clearly:** Foster open dialogue and ensure mutual understanding.
- **Build Rapport:** Use humor, shared experiences, and genuine interest to strengthen relationships.

2. The Impact of Emotional Intelligence on Leadership

Managers with high EI are better equipped to handle team dynamics, resolve conflicts, and inspire their teams. Emotional intelligence fosters trust, which is essential for effective collaboration.

Example:
A manager notices a team member is unusually quiet during meetings. Instead of assuming disengagement, the manager has a one-on-one conversation to check in. They discover the team member is dealing with a personal challenge and adjust their workload temporarily, ensuring both support and productivity.

3. How to Develop Emotional Intelligence
1. Practice Mindfulness:

Mindfulness helps you stay present and aware of your emotions. Techniques like meditation, deep breathing, or journaling can improve self-awareness and self-regulation.

2. Role-Play Scenarios:

Engage in exercises that simulate challenging conversations or conflicts. Practice listening and responding empathetically to develop social skills.

3. Observe and Learn:

Pay attention to emotionally intelligent leaders around you. How do they handle stress, deliver feedback, or navigate conflicts?

4. Commit to Ongoing Growth:

Recognize that EI is a skill that evolves with practice. Regularly revisit your emotional responses and refine your strategies for managing them.

4. Key Tips for Building Emotional Intelligence

- **Be Patient with Yourself:** Developing EI is a journey that requires practice and self-compassion.
- **Focus on the Team's Emotional Climate:** Pay attention to how team members interact and address issues that hinder collaboration.
- **Celebrate Progress:** Acknowledge even small steps in improving your EI to stay motivated.

Developing emotional intelligence strengthens your ability to lead with empathy, connect with your team, and navigate the complexities of leadership. By prioritizing this skill, you enhance not only your own growth but also the success and well-being of those you lead.

Balancing Authority and Empathy

As a manager, you must strike a balance between asserting authority and leading with empathy. Too much emphasis on authority can make you seem unapproachable, while an over reliance on empathy may undermine your ability to enforce boundaries and make tough decisions. The key lies in integrating both qualities to foster respect, trust, and effective leadership.

1. Establish Clear Boundaries

Authority doesn't mean micromanaging; it means setting clear expectations and holding the team accountable. Boundaries ensure that everyone understands their roles and responsibilities.

Key Strategies:

- **Communicate Non-Negotiables:** Be transparent about expectations, deadlines, and performance standards.
- **Stay Consistent:** Apply rules and policies fairly across the team.
- **Address Issues Promptly:** When standards aren't met, address them constructively and immediately.

Example:

A manager notices a team member consistently missing deadlines. Instead of letting it slide or being overly harsh, they have a candid conversation about the issue, reiterating expectations and offering support to identify obstacles.

2. Show Empathy Without Losing Authority

Empathy allows you to connect with your team, understand their challenges, and offer support. However, it's essential to maintain professionalism and ensure that empathy doesn't compromise accountability.

CHAPTER 5: PERSONAL GROWTH AS A MANAGER

Key Strategies:

- **Acknowledge Challenges:** Recognize when team members are struggling and offer resources or adjustments where appropriate.
- **Stay Solutions-Oriented:** Pair empathy with action by working collaboratively to address challenges.
- **Lead with Fairness:** Ensure that empathetic actions are balanced with maintaining team standards.

Example:
A team member struggles to adapt to a new project management tool, resulting in delays. The manager acknowledges the challenge and asks if it would be helpful to have a mentor assigned. The mentor's role is not to complete the tasks but to provide immediate training and answer questions as they arise. This approach balances empathy by offering support and maintaining accountability by ensuring the team members remain responsible for their deliverables.

3. Foster Mutual Respect

Balancing authority and empathy fosters an environment of mutual respect, where team members feel valued and supported while understanding the importance of accountability.

Key Strategies:

- **Listen Actively:** Make team members feel heard by engaging in meaningful conversations.
- **Model Respect:** Demonstrate respectful behavior in all interactions, especially during disagreements.
- **Recognize Efforts:** Acknowledge contributions regularly to reinforce a culture of appreciation.

Example:

During a conflict between two team members, the manager mediates by actively listening to both sides, addressing the issue impartially, and guiding them toward a collaborative resolution.

4. Key Tips for Balancing Authority and Empathy

- **Be Firm but Fair:** Stand by your decisions while remaining open to feedback and flexibility.
- **Separate Emotion from Action:** Lead with empathy but ensure decisions are driven by team goals and organizational needs.
- **Reinforce Accountability:** Empathy should never excuse repeated under performance. Balance support with clear consequences when necessary.

Balancing authority and empathy is an art that evolves with practice. By leading with both qualities, you inspire trust, create a positive work environment, and drive your team to excel. However, as a manager, you must also recognize when a situation cannot be corrected or changed. If a team member consistently fails to meet expectations despite support and guidance, it may be necessary to make a hard decision to let them go. This is never easy, but for the good of the team and the organization, such steps are sometimes required to ensure the team remains strong and productive.

Conclusion

Creating Your Custom Toolbox

As a manager, your journey is shaped by the tools you choose to use and how effectively you apply them. This book has provided strategies, insights, and exercises to help you grow into a leader who inspires, empowers, and drives results. The next step is to create your own "Management Toolbox" tailored to your unique style, team, and organization.

1. Reflect on Your Leadership Journey

Take time to evaluate where you are as a manager and where you'd like to grow. Ask yourself:

- Which areas of leadership do I excel in?
- Where do I face the most challenges?
- How can I apply the tools from this book to overcome those challenges?

By identifying your strengths and opportunities for growth, you can focus on the tools that will have the greatest impact.

2. Build Your Custom Toolbox

A great manager adapts their approach based on the situation and team. Use this book as a foundation to create a personalized set of tools and strategies.

Essential Tools to Include:

- **Goal-Setting Techniques:** Use SMART goals to create clarity and focus for your team.
- **Communication Skills:** Master active listening, clear messaging, and feedback delivery.
- **Conflict Resolution Strategies:** Turn challenges into opportunities for growth.
- **Motivation Methods:** Inspire your team through recognition, empowerment, and vision.
- **Time Management Approaches:** Optimize your day and help your team stay on track.

Add or modify tools as you gain experience and encounter new challenges. Your toolbox should evolve alongside your leadership journey.

3. Embrace the Hard Truths of Leadership

Leadership is rewarding, but it comes with difficult decisions and moments of uncertainty. Remember:

- Not every team member will align with your vision, and letting go of someone for the good of the team is sometimes necessary.
- Mistakes are inevitable; what matters is how you learn and grow from them.
- Leading by example and staying authentic builds trust and resilience within your team.

These truths remind us that leadership is as much about perseverance as it is about strategy.

4. Foster a Culture of Growth

As a leader, your influence extends beyond your own growth, it shapes the culture of your team and organization. Encourage your team to embrace learning, collaboration, and accountability. When you model these values, you create an environment where success becomes a shared goal.

5. A Final Thought

Leadership is not a destination but a journey. As you navigate the challenges and triumphs of management, remember that growth takes time, effort, and intention. Reflect often, adapt as needed, and celebrate your progress along the way.

Your "Management Toolbox" is now in your hands—use it to empower your team, achieve your goals, and leave a lasting impact on those you lead.

The Long-Term Impact of Effective Leadership

Leadership isn't about the immediate results you achieve, it's about the enduring legacy you leave behind. Effective leadership creates ripples that extend far beyond individual projects or goals. By investing in your growth and the development of your team, you build a foundation for success that stands the test of time.

1. The Power of Empowered Teams

A strong leader cultivates empowered teams that thrive even in their absence. By equipping team members with the skills, confidence, and autonomy to make decisions, you create a resilient and self-sufficient group capable of overcoming challenges.

Key Takeaway:

Empowered teams don't just meet expectations; they exceed them, driving innovation and collaboration that push the organization forward.

2. Developing Future Leaders

One of the greatest impacts a manager can have is fostering the growth of future leaders. When you mentor, coach, and support your team members, you contribute to a culture of leadership development that benefits the organization for years to come.

Key Takeaway:

Leadership is a legacy. The time and effort you invest in others will inspire them to do the same, creating a continuous cycle of growth and excellence.

3. Building a Positive Work Culture

The culture you shape as a leader affects the daily lives of your team members. A culture grounded in trust, communication, and collaboration not only enhances productivity but also contributes to the well-being and satisfaction of your team.

Key Takeaway:

Great leaders inspire great cultures, which attract and retain top talent, creating a thriving environment for success.

4. Your Personal Growth as a Leader

Leadership is as much about your own growth as it is about the development of your team. By committing to continuous learning, embracing challenges, and reflecting on your experiences, you ensure that your leadership evolves to meet the demands of an ever-changing world.

Key Takeaway:
The best leaders never stop growing. Your willingness to adapt and improve is the cornerstone of your long-term impact.

A Final Reflection

Effective leadership isn't about perfection—it's about progress. Each decision you make, challenge you face, and connection you foster contributes to the bigger picture of your leadership journey. By applying the principles and strategies in this book, you not only enhance your ability to lead but also create a positive and lasting influence on those you work with.

Leadership is your opportunity to inspire, empower, and transform. Embrace the journey, and let your impact resonate far into the future.

A Final Request

Thank you for joining me on this journey to build your "Management Toolbox." I hope this book has provided you with valuable insights and actionable strategies to enhance your leadership skills and inspire your team.

If you found this book helpful, I would be deeply grateful if you could take a moment to leave a positive review. Your feedback not only helps other readers discover the book but also ensures I can continue creating resources that empower managers like you.

Your review is a meaningful way to share the impact of this book and help others on their own leadership journey. Thank you for your time, your trust, and your commitment to becoming the best leader you can be.

A Note from the Author

I don't know where you are on your journey to becoming a great leader, but I sincerely hope this book has inspired you to reflect on and refine your management toolbox. If some tools are missing, I encourage you to begin cultivating them. If others are broken, take the time to repair them.

The principles and strategies shared here have been the foundation of my own management process—not just at work, but in everyday life. I believe in people and their capacity to grow. I also believe that, in any moment, we are all doing the best we can with the tools we have.

As you move forward, I wish you great success. You will experience both triumphs and setbacks along the way. It's all part of the journey. Let me leave you with one final thought to carry with you:

"Fear of failure is the kiss of death in the courtship of success."

Go forward with courage, curiosity, and confidence.

Acknowledgments and Sources

- *"The day you plant the seed is not the day you eat the fruit."* – **Fabienne Fredrickson**. This insightful quote has been included to emphasize the importance of patience and consistent effort in leadership growth.

www.ingramcontent.com/pod-product-compliance
Lightning Source LLC
Chambersburg PA
CBHW071109240526
45469CB00006BD/2397